Madhurashtakam

Madhurāṣṭakam

मधुराष्टकम्

Swami Tejomayananda

Central Chinmaya Mission Trust, Mumbai

First Edition - September 2010 - 5000 copies

•

Published by:

Central Chinmaya Mission Trust

Sandeepany Sadhanalaya

Saki Vihar Road, Mumbai 400072, India

Tel.: +91-22-2857 2367, 2857 5806

Fax: +91-22-2857 3065

Email: ccmtpublications@chinmayamission.com

Website: www.chinmayamission.com

•

Distribution Centre in USA:

Chinmaya Mission West

Publications Division

560 Bridgetown Pike

Langhorne, PA 19053, USA

Tel.: (215) 396-0390 Fax: (215) 396-9710

Email: publications@chinmaya.org

Website: www.chinmayapublications.org

•

Illustrations done by:

Sandeep Deshpande

•

Designed by:

Chinmaya Kalpanam, CCMT Publications

•

Printed by:

JAK Printers Pvt. Ltd.

•

Price: ₹ 200/-

ISBN 978-81-7597-497-5

Preface

It is beyond human comprehension to define or describe the personality of Lord Kṛṣṇa who encompasses the whole universe as revealed in *Śrīmad Bhagavad-gītā*. Yet Vallabhācārya, being a distinguished poet, scholar and an ardent lover of Lord Kṛṣṇa has brought out the most lovable aspects of the enchanting personality of Lord Kṛṣṇa in his immortal composition, *Madhurāshtakam*.

We are fortunate that Pūjya Guruji, Swami Tejomayananda has rendered exhaustive explanations of this Sanskrit composition in simple English, for the common man to perceive the sweetness of a divine form that heals and nourishes us. The discourses given by Pūjya Guruji in USA in 2009, form the text of this book.

CCMT has great pleasure in publishing this commentary on *Madhurāshtakam* and appreciates the substantial contribution of Brni Vividisha Chaitanya in editing the text.

We hope this divine theme will enrich the lives of devotees round the world with sweetness and devotion.

Śrī Gaṇeśa Caturthī
11th September, 2010
Mumbai

Central Chinmaya Mission Trust
Publications Division

Vallabhācārya

Śrī Vallabhācārya occupies a unique place in the Hindu Vaiṣṇava tradition as a scholar, philsopher and above all, as an ardent lover and propagator of the Bhāgavata Dharma.

It is seen that the advent of such a luminary is foretold by auspicious omens and miracles. Yoganārāyaṇa Bhatta, a Telugu Vaidiki brahmin and an ancestor of Vallabhācārya lived in Andhra Pradesh. According to devotional accounts, Śrī Kṛṣṇa Himself promised Yoganārāyaṇa that He would incarnate as a saint in his family if 100 somayajñas were performed.

Yoganārāyaṇa's descendant, Lakṣamaṇa Bhatta, who resided in Varanasi in the 15th century performed 100 yajñas, after which his wife Illammā conceived. At that point of time, Northern and Central India was subject to Muslim invasions. People were forced to flee sporadically to escape from religious persecution and conversion. It was precisely for these reasons that Lakṣamaṇa Bhatta had to move out of Varanasi, with his pregnant wife, Illammā.

Due to the strain and pain she suffered, she delivered a premature still-born baby. The distraught couple who did not have the heart to bury the baby placed him under a tree and moved on with heavy hearts. It was then that Lord Kṛṣṇa assured them that He was waiting for them under that very tree. They rushed back to that very spot and found the baby smiling in a circle of fire. The mother instinctively extended her arms into the fire. Both mother and son were unscathed. The baby was named 'Vallabha' meaning 'Beloved one'.

Vallabha was an exceptionally brilliant child, who soon gained mastery over the Vedas and the various systems of philosophy. His incredible achievements earned him the title of 'Bāla Sarasvati'. He earned the reverence of both Hindu and Muslim kings like Kṛṣṇadevarāya and Sikandar Loḍhi for his piety, purity and knowledge. In fact, the latter was so impressed by the saint that he got his court artist, Honāhar to paint his portrait and had it put up in one of the main palace halls.

With all the spiritual maturity and devotion this master had, he founded the Puṣti mārg, 'puṣti' meaning 'nourishment' and 'mārg' meaning 'path'.

The idea is that love of the Lord increases one's soul power. A follower of this path treats Bālakṛṣṇa or Laddu Gopāla like a real baby. Lāla is woken up with morning rāgas, bathed, decked up, given toys to play with, fed and put to sleep with lullabies. This tradition is enriched with the worship of the Lord through music, festivals, food, and so on.

After extensive padayātrās and sevā of the Lord and His devotees, Vallabhācārya took jala samāḍhi on the banks of the Gaṅgā in Kashi on the Rathayātrā day in 1531A.D.

Introduction

What is it in your life or this world that attracts or captivates your mind?

Please mull over this. You are all blessed with sense organs. When you see a thing of beauty—it could be the sunrise, the sunset, the rainbow or snow-clad mountains, the blue oceans or a valley of flowers, or then it could be a sweet, chubby child, a handsome man or a pretty woman—they please your eyes and attract your attention immediately.

Then again, your ears are drawn to pleasant sounds. Say, the sounds one hears at dawn, the chirping of birds, the blowing of the wind, the gush of the river, the cuckoo's call or a musician's riyaaz (practice)—these sounds hypnotize you by virtue of their melody. So what is pleasant and beautiful gives you joy.

What then to talk of delicious food! Its aroma tempts you before you actually eat it and the food itself melts in your mouth. Ah! There you are—already thinking of your favourite ice cream or chocolate or your favourite sweet.

So, the forms or colours you see, the food you eat, the sounds you hear, the fragrance you smell and the different sensations of touch—the hot stuffy air, the cool breeze or shower, all attract you, please you and give you joy.

But is it merely sense organs and their perceptions delight you? What about a humorous thought or an inspiring, noble one? A single such thought changes the course of your life and transforms you completely. Quotes like 'If you don't stand for something, you fall for everything,' leave an impression on our minds.

What to talk of feelings then? When you are in distress and you find a person sympathizing and empathizing with you, don't you feel better after you have opened up to him? As you think, so you become. If a person thinks sweet thoughts, that person becomes a sweet person and bitter thoughts make for a bitter person.

Thus we find that sense objects, emotions and feelings — all these can be gross or subtle, and fill us with bitterness or sweetness.

All that attracts you, pleases you, delights you, all that you find sweet and beautiful is summed up in a single Sanskrit word— 'madhu'.

Meaning of Madhu

If you look up to this word in a Sanskrit dictionary, the first meaning you find would be honey, meaning very sweet, very pleasant, delightful and attractive. An Upaniṣad-mantra says, 'jihvā me madhumattamā'—may my tongue be sweet. The Ṛṣis pray thus, 'madhu maniṣye madhu janiṣye madhu vakṣyāmi madhu vadiṣyāmi madhumatīṁ'—I think sweetly, create sweetly, speak sweetly and create sweetness! Creating sweetness doesn't mean becoming a confectioner of a diabetic patient! It means, that I will think sweet thoughts and this sweetness will rub off on all my family members. So when we speak to each other we don't spew bitterness and hurt one another.

Some people are experts, when it comes to insulting others. If you tell them 'You hurt my feelings,' their sarcastic reply will be, 'Oh! You have feelings too?' Or again, try telling such people, 'You disturbed my line of thought.'They are bound to shoot back, 'Ah! You think? Since when?'

Such speech is insulting and hurting. These days an atmosphere of distrust looms large in the world, be it between individuals, families, societies or nations.

When you land at any airport, there is a big 'welcome' board greeting you. But all this lasts only till you reach the immigration or customs counter. Then you realize how welcome you are!

On the other hand, if a person's thoughts, feelings and speech are sweet—in short his whole personality is permeated by sweetness, we are naturally attracted to such people. We seek their company, because they are full of madhu.

If madhu means beauty, sweetness, attraction and joy, then what is 'madhuram'? It is like this. If there is beauty and joy, there must be a source for all this madhu we experience. In fact, it must be a vast source—a śobhā sāgara—an ocean of beauty. That ultimate source is, what or whom we call Madhurādhipati—the Lord or giver of sweetness.

A great spiritual ācarya and devotee of the Lord, Śrī Vallabhācārya composed this lyrical hymn in praise of Lord Kṛṣṇa.

He opens our eyes to the fact that everything about the Lord is beautiful, pleasing, sweet, joy-giving and attractive. Therefore meditation on that Lord will naturally fill our whole being with joy.

Don't you like to be around people who smile? Some of us forget to smile, others smile to forget. The former are pessimists, the latter optimists. But both make it a point to smile when the photographer is clicking their pictures! This shows, that joy attracts us.

Here's an exercise for you. Sit in a room, all alone and think of someone you love. What happens? Watch. Next, change your mental make-up, and think of someone you dislike, or someone who dislikes you. Wouldn't you want to break the first thing you can lay your hands on, as a symbolic act of breaking the head of that person?

Vallabhācārya says, 'Well, here is the Lord, who is the embodiment of beauty and joy, and each and everything about him is sweet—madhurādhipaterakhilaṁ madhuram.' The Lord has two aspects: one is formless and the other is with form.

As the formless Lord, he is the very source of all beauty, sweetness and joy. But if you fail to see Him in creation, you can at least think of Him in a particular form that appeals to you.

But please don't limit Him to that form alone. That will make you a fanatic. So although this hymn talks of Lord Kṛṣṇa, you can extend it to any other form as well.

This hymn goes by the name *'Madhurāṣṭakam'*. Madhura means sweet and aṣṭakam means eight. So we have a set of eight verses on the Lord of sweetness.

Verse 1

अधरं मधुरं वदनं मधुरं नयनं मधुरं हसितं मधुरम्।
हृदयं मधुरं गमनं मधुरं मधुराधिपतेरखिलं मधुरम्॥१॥

adharaṁ madhuraṁ vadanaṁ madhuraṁ
nayanaṁ madhuraṁ hasitaṁ madhuram,
hṛdayaṁ madhuraṁ gamanaṁ madhuraṁ
madhurādhipaterakhilaṁ madhuram. (1)

The Lord here appears in a very captivating form. The verse begins by saying his lips are sweet.

Virtues are the ornaments of beauty and the ornaments of virtues are wisdom and knowledge. If a virtuous soul is devoid of wisdom, then he will be found wanting in beauty. So a Sanskrit reading goes –

> नरस्याभरणं रूपं रूपस्याभरणं गुणः ।
> गुणस्याभरणं ज्ञानं ज्ञानस्याभरणं क्षमः ॥
>
> *narasyābharaṇaṁ rūpaṁ rūpasyābharaṇaṁ guṇaḥ,*
> *guṇasyābharaṇaṁ jñānaṁ jñānasyābharaṇaṁ kṣamaḥ.*

The ornament for man is beauty, and that of beauty is wisdom. When a man reaches a state of perfection, and is yet patient with the imperfections of those around him, that is, when he is not critical or contemptuous of them, then we say that wisdom adorns him.

***Adharaṁ madhuraṁ*: Sweet are His lips!**

Paramātmā's is an eternally arresting smile. His smile is an ornament in itself. Our face gains additional beauty and value, when we smile.

***Vadanaṁ madhuraṁ*: His face is Sweet!**

The Lord is the source of all beauty. So naturally, His looks are the high-point of purity and perfection. The very sight of Him invokes joy and peace. Have you ever come across an idol or picture where Kṛṣṇa is weeping? When a seeker is absorbed in prayer and worship, the Lord's peace and joy gets reflected in his face too.

The great saint of Tāmilnāḍu Śrī Rāmānujācārya once met a man besotted with his wife's charm. "Brother, believe me, I have seen someone who surpasses your wife in beauty and charm. Come with me and see for yourself," said the saint.

The curious man followed the saint to a temple, where Lord Raṅganātha was bedecked in all splendour with jewels, flowers and candana. The radiance and divinity on His face was enough to transform the man into an ardent devotee.

In good times and bad times, make it a habit to gaze at the face of the Lord and soak in the joy and sweetness He radiates.

***Nayanaṁ madhuraṁ*: His eyes are beautiful!**

A lot of literature is devoted to the beauty and shape of eyes. But the real beauty of eyes is, when they radiate love and compassion.

The Sanskrit word for eye is 'nayanaṁ', and it comes from the root word 'ni', which means 'to lead'. Is it not true, that the eyes lead us to our destination?

In India, truck drivers have a phrase painted on the truck bumpers, which says, 'Dekho magara pyār se!' It means, 'Look, but look with affection.' The idea is, when you are caught in traffic, and there's a truck blocking your path, the truck driver won't let you overtake easily. He wants some fun at your expense.

But if you still manage to speed ahead, you would want to glare at the truck driver. Hence the phrase, 'Dekho magara pyār se!'

***Hasitaṁ madhuram*: His laughter is sweet!**

Demons guffaw in excitement. But their laughter is far from attractive. When you laugh at someone's downfall or misfortune, it is not madhura. But laughter that springs from affection and compassion is madhuram.

It is said in our śāstras, that the Lord's smile can either delude us or rid us of our delusions. The Lord's smile is so captivating, that you will immediately lose your heart to Him.

In the second chapter of the *Bhagavad-gītā*, we see how Lord Kṛṣṇa clears all the delusions of Arjuna by beginning his sermon with a smile!

***Hṛdayaṁ madhuraṁ*: His heart is beautiful!**

There are large-hearted people and then there are those with enlarged hearts!

A large heart is suffused with sweetness like the infinite space; an accommodating heart excludes none and includes one and all. This we see in the lives of enlightened masters and incarnations.

There is this incident in the Bible where people were stoning Mary Magdalene, because she was a sinner. Jesus Christ, who happened to be passing by at that moment, intervened to say, "Let the one who is without sin cast the first stone". Of course, none had the purity of heart save Jesus.

Even when nailed on the cross, Jesus had the magnanimity to plead for the very evildoers who tormented him, "Lord, forgive them for they know not what they do!" This indeed is hṛdayaṁ madhuraṁ—the sweetness of the heart

Gamanaṁ madhuraṁ: Sweet is His gait!

'Gamanaṁ' means 'walking' or 'going'. The Lord's ordinary everyday activities are madhuram too.

Have you seen the way people walk in anger? They stomp from one end of the room to the other, thump on the floor and kick the door—such is their gamanam. They smash things and push people. In a very broad sense, we could include gamanam to mean driving as well. People, who drive in anger, drive into danger. They dash into a lamppost or a garbage can and finally into a cyclist! When the police pull them up, and ask to see their license, they say as a matter of fact, "Are you kidding? Will anyone give me a license with this kind of driving?"

One should tread softly and with dignity, but the best gamanam is, when one rushes to save the distressed and suffering. Bhagavān sped to his devotees' side, when they called out to him in distress. Gajendra, the elephant, and Draupadi of Mahābhārata are but a couple of examples.

Madhurādhipaterakhilaṁ madhuram: Everything about the Lord of sweetness is sweet!

Once you get a glimpse of the Lord's sweetness, then it is for you to contemplate on that. What is it in certain people, that draws others to them? That is the madhuram in them. Even if a little of the Lord's madhuram rubs off on us, we will be blessed.

Verse 2

वचनं मधुरं चरितं मधुरं वसनं मधुरं वलितं मधुरम्।
चलितं मधुरं भ्रमितं मधुरं मधुराधिपतेरखिलं मधुरम्॥ २॥

vacanaṁ madhuraṁ caritaṁ madhuraṁ
vasanaṁ madhuraṁ valitaṁ madhuram,
calitaṁ madhuraṁ bhramitaṁ madhuraṁ
madhurādhipaterakhilaṁ madhuram. (2)

***Vacanaṁ madhuraṁ*: Sweet are His utterances!**

What He speaks, and how He speaks, both are beautiful. You and I talk sweetly too—but only to get our work done! Sometimes people talk sweet to others merely to stab them in the back later on.

But the sweetness of the Lord's words is enduring. It rids one of distress and delusion, like it did to Arjuna.

Your speech is madhuram, when it enlightens somebody, when your advice saves someone from danger, when it fills another's heart with love, devotion and wisdom. Mere empty flowery speech is not madhu, it is deceit.

A man living in Mumbai once assured his Delhi-based friend, "Whenever you are in need, just call me on the phone." Those were the days of trunk calls, when cell phones were not in vogue. So one day, the Delhi based man made a trunk call to his friend in Mumbai, "I am in need of 20,000 rupees. Please help me."

The Mumbai friend feigned inaudibility. "What did you say? I can't hear a word. The line is not clear." Both the men were shouting into the mouth of the telephone, when finally the operator came on the line, and told the Mumbai man, "Why do you say the line is not clear? The caller is asking you for 20,000 rupees!"

The Mumbai man retorted, "If you can hear him, you give him 20,000!"

So, his promise of being just a phone call away for a friend in need was meaningless.

When you speak, what you mean, and mean, what you speak, you are not mean! When you console, and enlighten another, your words are madhu; your speech is madhuram.

***Caritaṁ madhuraṁ*: His character is beautiful!**

When money is lost, nothing is lost. When time is lost, something is lost. When character is lost, everything is lost!

But we are prone to worrying about character the least, and money the most. All I hear is, "Svāmiji, the share market has crashed, the sensex is down, world economy has hit rock bottom!" None of us seem to worry about values crashing down!

When anyone makes money, by whichever way, he thinks he is successful. A man told his friend, "I made a million dollars!"

Astonished, his friend exclaimed, "Honestly?"
The man replied, "Let us not get into details!"
This is far from madhuram.

***Vasanaṁ madhuraṁ*: His clothes are beautiful!**

The Lord dresses Himself in beautiful garments. Beautiful? Sure. Expensive? No.

I think, Mahātmā Gandhiji wore the most appealing clothes. The British called him a half-naked fakir but Gandhiji, being a Mahātmā, wore a simple white dhoti, because he felt oneness with the impoverished masses of India. 'When majority of Indians lack clothes even to cover themselves, I don't have the right to wear costly clothes,' so felt the Mahātmā.

When Gandhiji had an appointment with the king of England, he went in his usual dhoti. When he was later questioned, as to how he felt sitting before the king clad in royal robes, the Mahātmā, quipped, "I felt perfectly okay, because his Majesty was wearing enough clothes for both of us!"

If a person wearing the best attire feels nothing for those around him in tatters, then his smart appearance is meaningless. This doesn't apply literally only to clothes. The question is, are all your possessions available to others? If they are, then alone is your vasanaṁ madhuram.

***Valitaṁ madhuram, calitaṁ madhuraṁ*: His whirling is sweet, and so is His conduct!**

Valitaṁ is movement, and calitaṁ is conduct. Character manifests in your actions, in your conduct.

When your conduct is great, then every word you utter, every thought you entertain, every emotion you feel is beautiful.

Man's brilliance may be evident in his extraordinary achievements, but his greatness is revealed in life's little things.

Kṛṣṇa's calitaṁ is beautiful. Caritraṁ is character and its expression in the form of actions and activities is the conduct of the person. An honest man's integrity is reflected in his behaviour—be it with his colleagues, friends or family. Thus a person's bearing is, what is called calitaṁ.

***Bhramitaṁ madhuraṁ*: His wanderings are sweet!**

Everything He did—even His wandering in the woods or moving around in the palace were sweet.

Our Paramaguru, Swami Tapovanjī mahārāja has authored a book titled '*Wandering in the Himālayas*'.

His treks in the Himālayas were undoubtedly beautiful, because through his travels he saw the joy and presence of the Divine in each and every thing—the mountains, the snow, the animals, the berries and birds.

But when we folks wander, we get lost! We are lost in the city, in the forest, and of course, if at all we happen to think! A man told his friend, "I got lost in my thoughts." His friend remarked, "Strange! I thought, that is an unknown territory for you!"

So, when we wander, we get lost. But when sages and saints wander about, they bring joy, wherever they go.

Try and bring joy, wherever you go, not whenever you go!

Verse 3

वेणुर्मधुरो रेणुर्मधुरः पाणिर्मधुरः पादौ मधुरौ ।
नृत्यं मधुरं सख्यं मधुरं मधुराधिपतेरखिलं मधुरम् ॥ ३ ॥

veṇurmadhuro reṇurmadhuraḥ
pāṇirmadhuraḥ pādau madhurau,
nṛtyaṁ madhuraṁ sakhyaṁ madhuraṁ
madhurādhipaterakhilaṁ madhuram. (3)

Veṇurmadhuro: *Sweet is His Flute!*

The flute is known by different names— murali, veṇu, vaṁśī—and each of these are variations of the same instrument. The sweetness, that the flute can produce, is in the hands of the flutist, literally too! When Kṛṣṇa plays the flute, He strikes the most mesmerizing notes on it, captivating the hearts of the devotees. In fact, it attracts all jīvas.

Vyāsa mahāmuni said of Lord Kṛṣṇa and his flute, *'niśamya gītaṁ tad anaṅgavardhanam vrajastriyaḥ kṛṣṇagṛhītamānasāḥ ājagmuḥ.'*

The Lord, standing on the banks of the Yamuna on the full moon night of Śarada-ṛtu (autumn), struck the most indescribable notes on his flute. All the gopis left their household chores halfway, and dashed to see Kṛṣṇa, with their minds so charmed. Symbolically, the Lord's music is a spiritual call.

When a jīva hears that call, then he or she forgets everything else, and cannot but follow the call of the Lord!

When Kṛṣṇa played on His flute, many didn't even hear His call. Perhaps they were listening to their mind's chatter. If our minds are preoccupied with our attachments and desires, how can we pay attention to the Lord's call?

But if you happen to hear it even once, you cannot ignore it. You follow Him helplessly as if under a spell! The beauty of the spiritual call is, that it liberates you.

The gopis and gopas were jealous of the flute. They wondered, 'What are the merits acquired by this flute, that He always keeps it with Him, and that too, close to His lips?'

The flute is made out of the bamboo reed. The bamboo shoots brave heat, chill and rain. Moved by their penance, the Lord chose them as material for His flute.

Also remember, the flute is one instrument that is completely hollow, and people pierce through it to make holes.

The flute says, 'I did tapas in the form of a shoot. Then people dented me with holes. I was okay with that too. Then again, I surrendered myself in the hands of the Lord, allowing His music to flow through me!'

This explains how the veṇu has come to be the most beautiful instrument in the service of the Lord.

It is evident, that, if you make yourself hollow, the Lord will fill you with His melody.

Many a time, people feel diffident, when they are assigned jobs and responsibilities. Their diffidence expresses as, 'I don't know, if I'm capable of doing this or not. Maybe I lack the ability.'

But a heartwarming spiritual principle is, 'God does not see your ability or inability. He only sees your availability.' Make yourself available to the Lord, like the flute does. Then you will be all madhuram.

All the great sages, souls and devotees are like the flute. They make themselves available to the Lord for him to play his melody through them. That is why, we find the music of all such devotees irresistible.

***Reṇurmadhuraḥ*: Sweet is the dust He treads upon!**

'Reṇu' means the dust of the lotus feet of the Lord. How sacred and purifying it is!

In Rāmāyaṇa, Ahalyā, the wife of Gautama Ṛṣi was cursed to become a stone. But when the dust of Śrī Rāma's feet touched that stone, Ahalyā emerged out of it as a completely purified, divine being. Just imagine! Even the dust of the Lord's feet has that power and magic!

Sūrdāsa, a great devotee of Lord Kṛṣṇa says in one of his songs, 'How I wish I was the dust of Vrindavana, where the Lord roamed about barefoot. I would also have got a touch of those feet—how sad! I did not become the dust of Vrindavana!'

Why? Because the dust particles got the direct touch of the Lord's feet. And remember, anyone, who gets to touch the feet of the Lord, or a divine being, feels blessed.

In the material world, if you get an award from the hands of the President of the nation, you feel so fulfilled. You make it a point to tell others, 'You know, I shook hands with the President.' If the first citizen's touch is so special, what then to speak of the touch of the divine!

Any blessed soul, who experiences it, experiences sheer bliss. 'Sukhena brahmasaṁsparśam atyantaṁ sukhamaśnute'.

A single dust particle of the Lord's feet is so sanctifying, that it can turn the tides of your destiny.

Pāṇirmadhuraḥ*: *His hands are so beautiful!

Wherein lies the beauty of His hands? The Lord is ājānubāhu —His arms are exceptionally long, they reach right up to His knees!

A Mahātmā explains, 'The Lord's arms are that long to enable Him to comfortably embrace even a fat devotee.'

His heart is of course all-embracing, but His arms have to be long enough to embrace the whole world in His love!

A hand is not beautiful, because of its shape, or the bracelets, or finger rings embellishing it. The real beauty of the hands lies in its capacity to give freely to others. 'Dānena pāṇir na tu kaṅkaṇena'. The Lord is ever ready to envelope the whole world in his embrace, and lend a helping hand. That is the true beauty of hands.

***Pādau madhurau*:** *Sweet are His feet!*

Hindu tradition considers touching the feet of respected souls as a reverential gesture. Youngsters seek blessings at the feet of elders, and disciples worship the Guru's feet.

Feet actually are symbolic of the foundation—the principles on which you stand. Agreed, your head is important too, but you can't stand on it, except while doing the śīrṣāsana, and that, too, for a few minutes only! You, of course, can't walk standing on your head.

You stand on your feet. In fact, your feet support your entire structure. That is why, you say about a man of integrity, 'This man stands for his principles.'

Then again, where is one rooted? The Lord Himself is the very foundation of this universe, and the entire world is rooted in Him. So, His feet represent Knowledge, the very substratum of creation.

Also, His feet are ever ready to rush anywhere to help, and serve anyone. Therein lies their beauty. That explains, why all devotees want to remain at the feet of the Lord. But the egoistic want to sit on His head! The right place is at His feet alone.

***Nṛtyaṁ madhuraṁ*: The Lord's dance is sweet!**

Kṛṣṇa's rāsa-līlā on the banks of the river Yamuna on Śarada Pūrṇimā night with the gopis is very popular. The Lord was the centre of attraction, literally too, as He danced in the middle, with all the gopis whirling around Him. This was not a rock 'n' roll, or disco dance, or a filmi number.

Certain kinds of music, songs and dances only provoke, and invoke our baser instincts of lust, greed and so on. Certain other kinds of music, devoid of vulgarity, are reserved for celebrations like weddings and festivals.

The Lord's dance, however, is on a different plane of dignity altogether. It fills, and fulfils all levels of one's personality—physical, emotional, sensory, intellectual and spiritual. It is beyond any description. Lord Kṛṣṇa's dance was not motivated by any kind of desire. In fact, all those, who were part of His dance, became desireless, and felt fulfilled.

That makes His nṛtyaṁ madhuram. That is why, many beautiful songs are composed on the dance of the Lord. 'Nṛtya karata Jamunā tīra Kṛṣṇa gopiyon ke saṅga Śarada Pūrṇimā ke rāta...' His dance transports you to the bliss of realization of your own self, the Self of all beings.

***Sakhyaṁ madhuraṁ*: His friendship is also sweet!**

A friendless person is a miserable person. No friend, no joy. The most quoted saying on friendship is, 'A friend in need is a friend indeed!' I read another version of it: 'A friend in need is a friend to feed!'

I happened to hear something interesting the other day. One man asked another, "You must have heard that a friend in need is a friend indeed?" The other man craftily quipped, "Yes stranger!" He said so, because he sensed, what his friend was upto!

In contrast, The Lord is an unfailing friend who stands by you through the thick and thin of life. Every other friend is either selfish or incapable of helping you. After all, remember, he too is a mortal like any other.

And even if he is capable, he cannot be with you 24x7. But the Lord is ever there for you—right in your heart. In the *Bhagavad-gītā* Lord Kṛṣṇa says, 'Whosoever recognizes me as a friend and well-wisher of all beings, attains peace.'

In short, the Lord is ever present, and, what is more, He is most loving, most compassionate and most competent. There is no question of Him deserting you.

You must have heard the common story, 'Footprints'.

One night, a man dreamt, that he was walking along a beach with the Lord, and across the sky flashed scenes from his life. Each scene had two sets of footprints on the sand— one belonging to him and the other to the Lord.

But on some occasions, he could see only one set of footprints. Those were the most difficult and saddest times of his life. He complained to the Lord, "I don't understand, why you left me alone, when I needed you the most."

The Lord smiled and gently replied, "During your times of trial and suffering, when you see only one pair of footprints, I carried you in my arms."

That is the kind of friend the Lord is—He never forgets you. This is proved in the lives of Sudāmā, Arjuna and others.

Turn to the Lord, you will find the one and only true friend in Him. His friendship alone is sufficient. On the other hand, if you have 1000 friends, but no bonding with the Lord, then you will still be found wanting. This does not, of course, mean, that you make enemies of all. This only means, that the Lord should be the reference point of your friendship with all.

Verse 4

गीतं मधुरं पीतं मधुरं भुक्तं मधुरं सुप्तं मधुरम्।
रूपं मधुरं तिलकं मधुरं मधुराधिपतेरखिलं मधुरम्॥ ४॥

gītaṁ madhuraṁ pītaṁ madhuraṁ
bhuktaṁ madhuraṁ suptaṁ madhuram,
rūpaṁ madhuraṁ tilakaṁ madhuraṁ
madhurādhipaterakhilaṁ madhuram. (4)

Gītaṁ madhuraṁ: ***Sweet is His song!***

Here, song includes the ones sung by Him, and also the ones sung about Him—those that describe Him and His glory. The very first English translation of the *Bhagavad-gītā* was called 'The Song Celestial!'

The Gītā is indeed madhuram, because it not only entertains you, but enlightens you too. A song, that delights you, has only entertainment value. But if it enlightens, too, and fills your heart with great love, then it is madhuram.

So songs sung by the Lord, on the Lord and for the Lord are all madhuram.

Pītaṁ madhuraṁ: ***His (act of) drinking is sweet!***

It is said that the act of drinking performed by the Lord is madhuram too. 'Oh, the Lord too drinks?' you may ask. Yes, of course, He drinks—but only milk and water!

Bhuktaṁ madhuraṁ: ***His (way of eating) is a treat!***

The Lord's act of eating is madhuram!
Little Kṛṣṇa ran from one house to another stealing butter. The episodes of Him licking butter and gulping milk are delightful. Why?

All the food, we consider ours, is given to us by Him alone. He alone is the rightful owner and giver of everything, we call ours. When He accepts our offerings, it is we, who are blessed. That poor brāhmaṇa Sudāmā had only a few flattened (and borrowed) rice grains, which he hesitantly offered to the Lord. Kṛṣṇa accepted the same happily, and blessed him heartily.

From a worldly standpoint, Sudāmā's poverty vanished. The Lord gifted him a palatial house and a prosperous life. But the subtler thing to note here is, how the Lord felt about it all. 'I've taken something from Sudāmā, and I must give him something substantial'.

What does the Lord give us? He gives us Himself and His love. Our own attachments, possessiveness and ego restrain us from giving ourselves to Him freely. But the Lord, being so great, snatches the very things, we hold on to, and releases us from our bondages.

The way He rids us of our burdens is also sweet. Butter is the very essence of milk. It symbolizes love, affection and devotion. The essence of any karma you perform, is measured by the amount of love and devotion, you invest in it.

That is why, when someone serves you a sumptuous meal at their house, you ask, 'How did you make this delicious dish? What is the recipe?' Then the lady of the house says, 'The special ingredient I added is love. That made all the difference!'

Now, imagine a contrary scene. Suppose you are offered dinner in a very rude manner, 'Look! Here is the dinner. Eat, if you feel like.' Would you feel like tasting it, though it may be of great quality?

The episodes of the Lord and his gopabālas stealing butter show that He valued the love and devotion of people. If you get a chance to give something to somebody, do not hesitate, because the Lord comes to us in many forms—as a child, a beggar, a rich man or a needy man. Offer, what you want to, with love and respect, as if you are offering it to the Almighty Himself.

***Suptaṁ madhuram*: The Lord's sleep is beautiful!**

Your little one looks so sweet and innocent, while he is fast asleep. So you immediately get your camera, and click away to your joy. Then again, when the baby opens his eyes, you shoot a few more pictures.

Baby Kṛṣṇa was a picture of sweetness, as He opened His eyes, closed them in sleep, or pursed His lips.

The scene of mother Yaśodā, putting Him in the cradle and singing a lullaby to Him, is so heartwarming.

Sleep is all-important to one's health and life. People are forced to endure starvation of various kinds—hunger starvation and sleep starvation.

Hard work or heavy workload leaves them with sleeping problems. They then pop sleeping pills, that don't work.

One man shared his suffering with me, "Svāmījī, I take sleeping pills and still don't fall asleep, don't know what is wrong."

I explained, "You are taking sleeping pills, meaning your pills are sleeping. So, how will they work?"

I then suggested, "Please meditate on sleeping Bāla Kṛṣṇa at bedtime, then see how quickly you will fall asleep."

It is we mortals, who suffer from insomnia or sleep apnea. The Lord sleeps peacefully anywhere, anytime.

Do you know, where the sweetness of sleep lies? In its healing and refreshing energies.

A good night's sleep leaves you ready for work. But we wish 'sweet dreams' to those about to retire. We already daydream too much. Why dream in sleep too?

***Rūpaṁ madhuraṁ*: The Lord's form is so beautiful!**

In Rāma-stuti, Tulsidāsji says, the Lord is 'kandarpa agaṇita amita chhavi nava nīla nīraja sundaram.' We deck up with ornaments to look beautiful. The ornaments add to our appearance. But when the Lord is adorned with ornaments, it is the other way round—He adds beauty to them. The Lord's natural rūpam is so madhuram. He is vibhūṣaṇāṅgam.

***Tilakaṁ madhuraṁ*: His tilak is sweet!**

The candana mark on His forehead is called tilakam. When devotees visit temples, they apply a dot, a straight line, or a 'U' shaped tilaka on their foreheads.

For Hindu women, this dot, apart from being a beauty spot, is also a sign of auspiciousness. The spot where you put the bindi is the seat of remembrance. We apply tilaka in temples as a mark of remembrance of the Lord.

The Lord's candana tilaka highlights His beauty.

Verse 5

करणं मधुरं तरणं मधुरं हरणं मधुरं स्मरणं मधुरम् ।
वमितं मधुरं शमितं मधुरं मधुराधिपतेरखिलं मधुरम् ॥ ५ ॥

karaṇaṁ madhuraṁ taraṇaṁ madhuraṁ
haraṇaṁ madhuraṁ smaraṇaṁ madhuram,
vamitaṁ madhuraṁ śamitaṁ madhuraṁ
madhurādhipaterakhilaṁ madhuram. (5)

***Karaṇaṁ madhuraṁ*: All that he does is beautiful!**

An expert artist draws anything from a straight line to a circle with natural ease. Some of us cannot manage to draw a straight line even with a ruler or a circle with a compass! But an artist does it with effortless ease.

One of our Chinmaya camps was graced by a professional artist. He asked one of us to draw anything of our choice on the blackboard. A child drew two lines at a distance from each other, and the artist came up with an amazing picture around the lines making those lines a part of his drawing as well.

Then, even as we were chanting a hymn on Goddess Sarasvati, he drew a picture of her as described in the prayer. When we finished chanting, the picture was ready! So too, the initial note of any song, that an accomplished musician sings, will be madhuram.

I had the opportunity to live with a great soul, our Pūjya Gurudev Swami Chinmayananda. Every little thing he did—be it opening an envelope or sealing it or writing an address on its cover—bore a stamp of his beauty and grace. He left his unique mark on all his actions. Those, who do shoddy work, leave their mark too! Nobody else can perform like them!

Swami Vivekananda once remarked, that an isolated act of greatness does not establish a person's mettle. Real greatness reflects in every act, a person does, be it small or big. Every action of the Lord is spellbinding; to begin with, His creation is marvellous. When the Lord incarnated as Kṛṣṇa, every action of His—be it playing on the flute, dancing with the gopis, walking or grazing the cows—was mesmerizing.

The way, He drove Arjuna's chariot in the battlefield, was a scene worth watching. And in His duty as charioteer, He took it upon Himself to bathe the horses, massage their limbs, clean and heal their wounds.

He could have easily appointed someone else for these tasks. But He took complete charge, and did full justice to His role as charioteer.

All His actions were graceful, since they were unselfishly performed for the common good of all.

That is why, people longed to see Him, as He went about walking, singing or playing. Every movement of His, and every deed of His, heaped joy, bliss, peace, prosperity and goodness on mankind.

That made His karaṇam madhuram. His slaying of demons was madhuram too, because they were redeemed by Him.

***Taraṇaṁ madhuraṁ*: Lord's swimming is beautiful!**

Yamuna was a very toxic river at one point, thanks to the serpent Kāliyā. But Lord purified its waters by dancing on the many-headed serpent and subduing him.

At a deeper level, His taraṇam, His swimming or crossing the river is beautiful, because even as He swims, He helps countless souls cross the river of saṁsāra, with its dangerous waves of delusion and ignorance.

It is only an expert swimmer, who can save a drowning man. Anyone else mars the least chance of survival of the sinking man. The Lord alone knows, how to cross the river of saṁsāra, and, how to help others cross this turbulent river.

Haraṇaṁ madhuraṁ: *His manner of stealing is sweet!*

'Haraṇam' means 'to rob' or 'to steal'. But here it more appropriately means 'to take away'. If the Lord takes away something from you, it is for your own good. The Lord takes away many things, the subtlest of all being our ignorance, then our desires and our petty attachments. A beautiful story illustrates this point very well.

Kṛṣṇa and Arjuna were moving around in disguise. They happened to be near a rich man's house, when they felt famished. They knocked on the rich man's door for food. This annoyed the rich man, who cursed them. Kṛṣṇa, in turn, blessed him, saying, 'May you prosper.'

Next, Kṛṣṇa and Arjuna stopped by a poor man's hut. All that the poor man owned, was a cow and a calf. He was a devotee, immersed in singing the name of the Lord. His only food was the milk of the cow. Yet he welcomed them both, and lovingly offered them the milk, he was to drink. As they were taking leave of him, the Lord raised His hand in blessing, and told the old man, 'May your cow and calf die.'

This shocked Arjuna, who expressed his disapproval, "Kṛṣṇa, this is grossly unfair. You blessed the haughty rich man with prosperity, though he was so rude to us, and you are denying this kind old man his very source of sustenance!"

The Lord explained, "This old man is my devotee. This cow and calf are the only things standing between him and me; they distract him in his meditation. With their death, he will come to me. I gave the rich man only worldly prosperity. But to this old man, I am giving Myself."

This shows, that the Lord takes away something from us for our greatest good. He takes away your money, because you are too attached to it. When you get something, accept it as the Lord's blessing, and, if He takes it away, don't worry.

What you should feel then is, 'As long as the Lord is with me, everything is fine.' His taking away of our sorrows, our afflictions, and our bondages is madhuram.

***Smaraṇaṁ madhuraṁ*: Remembrance of the Lord is sweet!**

When we remember the Lord, it is madhuram. But suppose the Lord remembers us? In that case, it is nothing short of sheer bliss.

There is an episode in the Bhāgavatam, where Vidura meets Uddhava after Kṛṣṇa departs from this world. Vidura knows, that Kṛṣṇa has blessed Uddhava with divine Knowledge in the final moments of his exit. Vidura requests Uddhava to share this Knowledge with him. But Uddhava replies, "No, I won't. Because, before He left, Kṛṣṇa remembered you fondly, and instructed the great sage, Ṛṣi Maitreya, to give you this Knowledge." Vidura was moved to tears hearing this, because he felt, that among all the countless people in this world, the Lord had cared to think of him. So, your remembrance of the Lord, and His remembering you, are both madhuram.

***Vamitaṁ madhuraṁ śamitaṁ madhuraṁ*: Sweet is His love! – Sweet is His calm!**

Śamitam is the calm meditative state of the Lord, and vamitam is, when He gushes with love and affection. Both are madhuram.

When the Lord speaks, it is madhuram, and, when he is silent, that is madhuram too. In other words, we should all know, when to speak, and when to keep mum. This applies particularly to public speakers. They must be conscious of, when to begin a speech, how much to speak, and when to end their speeches.

One man spoke for what seemed like an eternity, and later asked his friend, "How did you find my discourse?"

His friend replied, "Your discourse was good, but you don't have to be eternal to be immortal!"

Later the speaker asked his wife for her candid comments on his lecture. Her feedback was, "The lecture was good, but you missed many opportunities, where you could have stopped." That is the reason, I keep a watch on my watch while giving a discourse. Otherwise the listeners will start watching their watches!

Another thing to note is that, whatever you say, must be meaningful.

A woman told her friend, "My husband can go on and on talking for hours on any topic." Her friend said, "My husband needs no topic to talk endlessly."

Speak, when you have something to say, not because you have to say something. And, when you have put your point across, keep quiet. Speech is beautiful, when it is meaningful and helpful.

Verse 6

गुञ्जा मधुरा माला मधुरा यमुना मधुरा वीची मधुरा।
सलिलं मधुरं कमलं मधुरं मधुराधिपतेरखिलं मधुरम्॥ ६॥

guñjā madhurā mālā madhurā
yamunā madhurā vīcī madhurā
salilaṁ madhuraṁ kamalaṁ madhuraṁ
madhurādhipaterakhilaṁ madhuram. (6)

Guñjā madhurā: *Sweet are the guñjā beads!*

Till now, the hymn is focussed on the Lord—His form, His limbs, His features, His deeds—all of which are madhuram.

Here, we have a list of things associated with the Lord, all of which are madhuram. Your world is made up of two things—you and yours. Similarly, we have the Lord and things associated with Him.

Look around, and you will see, that everything boils down to association. Suppose, a wealthy person wears an ornament, everyone gushes about it, 'Oh! What a beautiful pearl necklace! Wow! Such eye-catching rubies!' But, if you spot a beggar wearing the same ornaments, your first thought is, 'It must all be artificial jewellery.' And the second thought is, 'If it is real, it must definitely be stolen.'

So, though the ornament is the same, it appears real or fake depending on, whom it is associated with. Human nature is peculiar. When a rich man wears something, we admire him. When a poor man wears the same thing, we suspect him. Thus association makes all the difference.

Since the Lord is most beautiful and blissful, all things associated with Him are madhuram.

Guñjā is a reddish coloured bead. The garland made of guñjā is beautiful, because the Lord is wearing it, and Yamuna is also beautiful, since the Lord is standing on its banks.

Mālā madhurā: *His garland looks sweet!*

'Mālā' is a very nice word with a pun in it. One meaning of it is 'garland' and 'mā' also means Lakṣmī, the goddess of wealth, beauty and prosperity. So, the great goddess of wealth resides in the Lord's garland. That is why, the garland the priest gives you in the temple, is prasāda. The same mālā bought from the market, and worn on your person, carries no sacred significance.

***Yamuna madhurā*: Sweet flows the Yamuna!**

The Yamuna river's association with Lord Kṛṣṇa is perpetual. In Rāmacaritamānasa, Gosvāmi Tulsidāsa, while describing the demons and asuras of Rāvaṇa's Laṅkā says, 'I am making only a brief mention of them, because very soon, they will come in contact with Lord Rāma's arrows, and attain mokṣa.' But for their association with Lord Rāma, Tulsidāsa wouldn't have written even a word about the evil-minded demons.

In this world, everyone wants to associate himself or herself with a special someone. It all depends on, what you value in people. Some want to associate themselves with industrialists, some with sportsmen, some others with powerful politicians, and yet others with celebrities. But association with the Lord surpasses every other contact.

***Vīcī madhurā salilaṁ madhuraṁ*: Sweet are the waves and the water!**

All the waves of joy in the Yamuna are beautiful. Therefore, salilaṁ madhuram— even the water is sweet. As mentioned earlier, Kāliyā had polluted Yamunā with his poison. But the Lord purified the waters by dancing on Kāliyā and blessing him too, in the process.

***Kamalaṁ madhuram*: Sweet is the lotus!**

When the lotus blooms in the river, it adds beauty to the waters, and the water in turn sustains it.

Verse 7

गोपी मधुरा लीला मधुरा युक्तं मधुरं भुक्तं मधुरम् ।
दृष्टं मधुरं शिष्टं मधुरं मधुराधिपतेरखिलं मधुरम् ॥ ७ ॥

*gopī madhurā līlā madhurā yuktaṁ
madhuraṁ bhuktaṁ madhuram,
dṛṣṭaṁ madhuraṁ śiṣṭaṁ madhuraṁ
madhurādhipaterakhilaṁ madhuram. (7)*

Gopī madhurā: ***Sweet is His gopī!***

Cattle rearing, milking the cows and selling milk, are all part of a milkmaid's life. But, what made the gopīs of Vrindavana especially sweet? They were devotees of Lord Kṛṣṇa. They loved Him, and He, too, loved them.

'Go' in Sanskrit means 'sense organs' and 'pī' means 'to drink'. The gopīs were constantly drinking the beauty of Lord Kṛṣṇa with all their senses, not merely their eyes. And they were so full of Kṛṣṇa, that, even when they were selling milk, they said, 'Anyone for Kṛṣṇa?' instead of, 'Anyone for buying milk?'

The Lord's name came so naturally to them, that they forgot every other name — be it curd, milk or butter.

Līlā madhurā: ***Sweet is His sport!***

Līlā means sports. Each of the Lord's sports is beautiful. Līlā in Sanskrit is defined as 'līnaṁ bhāvaṁ lāti prākaṭyati'—that, which manifests a dormant emotion. Love for the Lord is always dormant in our hearts. But, when the Lord enacts His līlā, that love becomes manifest.

When you watch a film or play, the horror scenes and the comic ones arouse the sentiments of fear, laughter and so on, and we respond accordingly. That is what a līlā does. The Lord's līlās are such, that they bring out our love and devotion for Him, and they destroy all our clinging attachments. That makes His līlās madhurā.

Yuktaṁ madhuraṁ: ***Sweet is union with Him!***

'Yuktam' means union, and meeting with the Lord, is sweet. Longing for the Lord leads to darśana of Him. Then, there is a delightful union of Lord and devotee.

***Bhuktaṁ madhuram*: Sweet is the protection afforded by Him!**

This word appeared even earlier in this very hymn. There it meant, the act of eating. Here it means 'the joy of meeting the Lord'. Another meaning of 'bhuktaṁ' is 'protection'. Protection given to us by the Lord is sweet and long lasting.

There have been instances, where the bodyguard has kidnapped or killed his employer, whom he had to protect, risking his own life. But God offers true and lasting security and protection. So, a meeting with Him is madhuram, and being protected by Him, is a sweet experience too.

***Dṛṣṭaṁ madhuraṁ*: Sweet is His glimpse!**

Whatever is seen by the Lord, is beautiful, and, what you are able to see of the Lord, is also beautiful. Even a glimpse of His little finger is 'Ah! So beautiful!' Then, what to talk of the glimpse, that the Lord casts at you?

***Śiṣṭaṁ madhuraṁ*: Sweet is His gentleness!**

'Śiṣṭam' means obedience. One who is cultured, gentle, obedient, of pleasing mannerisms is a śiṣṭa puruṣa, a gentleman.

The Lord is a complete śiṣṭa puruṣa. Opposite of śiṣṭam is duṣṭam—wickedness. The Lord punishes and disciplines duṣṭa puruṣas, and protects sādhus.

Verse 8

गोपा मधुरा गावो मधुरा यष्टिर्मधुरा सृष्टिर्मधुरा ।
दलितं मधुरं फलितं मधुरं मधुराधिपतेरखिलं मधुरम् ॥ ८ ॥

gopā madhurā gāvo madhurā
yaṣṭirmadhurā sṛṣṭirmadhurā,
dalitaṁ madhuraṁ phalitaṁ madhuraṁ
madhurādhipaterakhilaṁ madhuram. (8)

***Gopā madhurā*: Sweet are His cowherd playmates!**

Not only were the women of Vrindavana sweet, but the men and children were madhuram, too. They were the lucky ones, most fortunate ones, blessed ones and privileged ones, because the Lord lived with them as one of them, and mingled, and played with them.

***Gāvo madhurā*: Sweet are His cows!**

Even the cows of Vrindavana were blessed, since the Lord used to drink milk directly from their udders. How lucky were the cows to enjoy the touch and caresses of the Lord Himself!

***Yaṣṭirmadhurā*: Sweet is His stick (with which He tends cows)! The cowherd's stick was also madhuram.**

The cowherds carried sticks to drive the cattle. 'Go' means cow; it also means our senses. For keeping the cattle in line, an ordinary stick would do. But to make our senses toe the line, you need the stick of discipline. Otherwise our senses may go wild. Therefore, the Lord wields a stick in one of His hands. 'Totra vetraika pāṇaye'—the Lord held a whip in one of His hands to direct the horses. The stick is necessary to make us behave ourselves.

But please note, that the cowherds used sticks just to guide their cows, not cane them. One can even look upon the scriptural injunctions as yaṣṭis to keep us on the track.

***Sṛṣṭirmadhurā*: His creation is sweet!**

God's creation is madhuram; it is man, who has polluted it.

Still, it manages to remain beautiful. The blue sky, the moon and the stars, the planets and satellites and the ocean—each of these by themselves, and all of these put together, are beautiful.

***Dalitaṁ madhuraṁ phalitaṁ madhuraṁ*: Sweet are leaves and ripe fruits blessed by Him!**

'Dalitam' means leaves and 'phalitam' means fruit. 'Dalitam' also means manifestations, and 'phalitam' also means joy. The Lord's joys, His jokes, His humour, are all beautiful.

Look around, and you will find beauty in trees, leaves, flowers and fruits. It is we, who spoil the Lord's creation with our petty likes and dislikes.

***Madhurādhipaterakhilaṁ madhuram*: All about the Lord of sweetness is sweet!**

This line is repeated as the last line in every śloka. This is to emphasize the fact, that everything about the Lord of Sweetness is sweet, beautiful, pleasing and attractive. Look at Him anyway you feel like. You will find Him to be sweetness personified.

This composition gives us direction for our thought process and guidelines for meditation. We offer our respects to the great poet-saint Śrī Vallabhācārya for giving us this priceless hymn to sing and meditate upon.

When we contemplate upon the form of the Lord or on anything that belongs to Him, we will find sweetness, beauty, love and light flowing into our lives, wiping away all bitterness.

This hymn can take us a few steps towards bettering our individual life and thereby the world around. A very thought-provoking quotation reads, 'Your inner beauty and purity is reflected in the smiles of the people around you.'

Madhurāṣṭakam, regularly chanted or meditated upon, can help us render that service. May God, Gurudev and Ācāryas fill our hearts with the beauty and purity, this hymn depicts.

Transliteration and Pronounciation Guide

In the book, Devanāgarī characters are transliterated according to the scheme adopted by the International Congress of Orientalists at Athens in 1912. In it one fixed pronunciation value is given to each letter; f, q, w, x and z are not called to use. An audio recording of this guide is available at http://chinmayamission.com/scriptures.php. According to this scheme:

Devanāgarī	Translit-eration	Sounds Like	Devanāgarī	Translit-eration	Sounds Like
अ	a	son	ढ्	ḍh	adhesive*
आ	ā	father	ण्	ṇ	under*
इ	i	different	त्	t	tabla
ई	ī	feel	थ्	th	thumb
उ	u	full	द्	d	this
ऊ	ū	boot	ध्	dh	Gandhi
ऋ	ṛ	rhythm*	न्	n	nose
ॠ	ṝ	**	प्	p	pen
ऌ	ḷ	**	फ्	ph	phantom*
ए	e	evade	ब्	b	boil
ऐ	ai	delight	भ्	bh	abhor
ओ	o	core	म्	m	mind
औ	au	now	य्	y	yes
क्	k	calm	र्	r	right
ख्	kh	khan	ल्	l	love
ग्	g	gate	व्	v	very
घ्	gh	ghost	श्	ś	shut
ङ्	ṅ	ankle*	ष	ṣ	sugar
च्	c	chuckle	स्	s	simple
छ्	ch	witch*	ह्	h	happy
ज्	j	justice	ं	ṁ	improvise
झ्	jh	Jhansi	ः	ḥ	**
ञ्	ñ	banyan	क्ष्	kṣ	action
ट्	ṭ	tank	त्र्	tr	three*
ठ्	ṭh	**	ज्ञ्	jñ	gnosis
ड्	ḍ	dog	ऽ	'	a silent 'a'

* These letters don't have an exact English equivalent. An approximation is given here.

** These sounds cannot be approximated in English words.

Books on General Topics by
Swami Tejomayananda

Right Thinking

Satyam Śivam Sundaram

Victorious Youth

Manaḥ Śodhanam

Vision of the Bhagavad-Gītā

You Ask, He Answers

Towards Greater Success

Hindu Culture

Parenting

Ponder Awhile

Meditation A Vision

The Game Of Life

Tips for Happy Living

Life of Vision

Pūjya Guruji Swami Tejomayananda is an outstanding teacher of Vedānta, with a profound depth beneath his simplicity and humility. He has a simple conviction – to fortify, strengthen and actualise the vision of his Guru, Pūjya Swami Chinmayananda.

Guruji has written commentaries on many Vedāntic texts. He has authored many original compositions on Vedānta and Bhakti (Devotion) and books on various other relevant topics.

He is the current head of the Chinmaya Mission – a global spiritual organisation with more than 250 centres worldwide.